Birds of the Air

By Arabella Buckley

Birds of the Air

Table of Contents

CHAPTER I: Birds We Know

I WONDER how many birds you know by sight, and what you could tell about their nests and their lives?

There are between three and four hundred different British birds, and very few people know them all. But in any one place there are not more common birds than you could learn in a year. You can look for the rare ones afterwards.

The best way to begin is to write down those you are sure about, and say how you recognise them. You cannot mistake a Robin, with his red breast, his plump little body, and his brown wings. The mother robin's breast is not quite so red, and the young have no red at all. But when you have seen them with the cock-robin, you will soon know them by their shape.

But a Chaffinch has a red breast. How can you tell him from a robin? His breast is much browner than the robin's, and even at a distance you may know him by the white bands on his dark wings, and the yellow tips to some of his feathers. Then his body is longer, and he moves more gracefully than the robin, while his loud *"pink, pink,"* if you go near his nest, will tell you at once what he is.

The Lark you know by his slender brown body and white speckled throat, and by the way he soars, as he sings his sweet song. The common green Woodpecker is easily known by his bright colours, his curious feet, and his stiff tail, which he uses to jerk himself up a tree. And though a Nuthatch also goes up a tree by jumps, you would never take him for a woodpecker, for he is no bigger than a sparrow, and he has a short tail and blue-grey wings and a dingy red breast.

Then you know the cooing Wood-pigeon, the chattering Magpie, the soaring Hawk and his hooked beak, and the downy Owl. And I daresay you could tell me of many more.

4

The birds you know best will most of them be with us all the year round. But not all. The Swifts fly away to the south in August, and the Swallows and the Martins follow in October. When they are gone the Fieldfares come from the north, and feed in flocks on the worms in the damp fields, and on the holly berries when the ground is hard with frost.

The Swallow and the House Martin are so alike that, as they come and go together, you might not know them apart, unless you remember that a Swallow has a blue-black collar across his breast, and that the fork of his tail is longer than that of the Martin. You may be busy all the year round watching the birds, seeing when they come and go, what food they eat, how they fly, whether they sing in the morning or evening, and where they build their nests.

Many farmers and gardeners shoot little birds because they eat their corn and peas and fruit. But a large number of birds feed chiefly on insects. You ought to know which these are, for they are very useful in clearing away earwigs and caterpillars, as well as slugs and snails. If you look out early some morning and see a Thrush tapping a snail-shell against a stone to get at the snail, you will say he is a good gardener. You will not grudge him a little fruit in the summer.

Then there are the nests and the young birds to watch. You need not take the nests, nor rob the birds of their eggs. You will learn much more by pulling back the leaves and the twigs, and peeping gently into the nest. For then you can come another day and watch when the eggs hatch, and how the young birds grow. If you are careful not to disturb the bush nor touch the eggs, the mother will not desert them. Last year a pair of Thrushes built their nest in a hedge by the side of a path where people were always passing. But though I went often to look at it, the mother brought up all her four little ones. She would even sit still on the nest when I peeped in, while her mate sang on a tree close by.

Point out and describe six birds common in the neighbourhood.

CHAPTER II: The Song of Birds

BIRDS sing when they are happy, and cry out when they are frightened, just as children do. Only they have songs and cries of their own. You can always tell when the little song-birds are happy, for each one trills out his joyous notes as he sits on a branch of a tree, or the top of a hedge.

In the early morning of the spring, you will hear singing in the garden almost before it is light. First there is a little chirping and twittering, as if the birds were saying "good-morning" and preparing their throats. Then, as the sun rises, there comes a burst of song.

Robins, Thrushes, Blackbirds, Chaffinches, and Wrens whistle away merrily, and many other little birds join in. While they are all singing together, it is not easy to tell one song from another, though the Thrush sings loudest and clearest of all.

Then they fly away to their breakfast and, as the day goes on, you hear one or two at a time. So you can listen to the notes of each song, and if you go near very quietly, you can see the throat of the bird swelling and quivering as he works the little voice-chords inside, which make the notes.

It is not easy to write down what a bird sings, for it is like whistling—there are no words in it. But people often try to imitate their songs in words. Listen to the Thrush. You can fancy he says "cherry-tree, cherry-tree, cherry-tree" three times. Then, after some other notes, he sings "hurry-up, hurry-up," and "go-it, go-it." For the thrush has a great many notes.

The pretty Yellowhammer, with its bright yellow head, sings "a little bit of bread, and no che-e-s-e." The Chiff-chaff calls "chiff-chaff, chiff-chaff" quite distinctly. Any child can imitate the cuckoo, or the coo-oo-oo of the wood-pigeon.

As the days grow hotter, the birds sing less. They sit on the branches of the trees, or on the hedges under the shade of the leaves, or hop about in the wood.

Then when the evening comes, and long shadows creep over the grass, each bird looks out for his supper. When he is satisfied he sings his evening song of content, before he goes to sleep.

What a concert it is! Finches, tomtits, sparrows, wrens, robins, and chaffinches all singing at once. And above them all, come the song of the thrushes and blackbirds, the cooing of the wood-pigeon and the caw-caw of the rooks as they fly home from the fields. As the thrushes were the first to begin in the morning, except the lark, so they are the last to leave off at night, and often one thrush will go on long after all the others are quiet.

Then at last all seem to have settled down for the night. But no! If you live in Kent, or any part of the south or east of England, you may hear in May or June a sweet sound, like a flute, coming softly from many parts of the wood. This comes from the Nightingales, who, in the warm summer, will sing nearly all night.

They sing in the day as well, but their note is so soft that often you cannot hear it when more noisy birds are singing. In the still night you can hear the sweet song rising up six notes and then bubbling like a flute played in water. When you have once heard a nightingale sing you will never forget it. In Yorkshire or Devonshire you will not hear him, for he does not go so far to the North or to the West.

Birds sing most in the spring, for then they are making their nests, and the father bird sings to the mother while she is building, and when she is sitting on the eggs. You may often find out where a Robin's nest is hidden by seeing the cock-robin sitting on a branch singing to his mate. Most people too, have seen the Wood-pigeon puffing out his throat and cooing and bowing to the mother bird on her nest. For pigeons make love all the year round.

When the mother bird is sitting, the father bird sings for joy, and when the young birds are hatched he teaches them his song. Song-birds have very delicate throats. They have muscles, which quiver like the strings of a violin, and the young birds have to learn to work these muscles.

It is curious to hear a young Blackbird or Thrush beginning to try a tune. First he sounds one note, then two or three. They are not always in tune, but he tries again and again. So little by little he learns his father's song.

Birds of the Air

Listen to the song of birds—robins, thrushes, blackbirds, larks, nightingales, bullfinches and others, and try to imitate them by whistling.

CHAPTER III: The Nests of Birds

IF you want to know how cleverly nests are made, you should collect a few which the birds have deserted, or from which the young birds have flown.

You will find a Hedge-sparrow's nest in many a hawthorn bush, and though it is a simple nest, I think you will find, if you pull it to pieces, that you cannot put it together again as well as the bird did.

A Chaffinch's nest is more finely woven. You will most likely find one in the apple trees in the orchard. It is made of dry grass and moss matted together with wool in the shape of a deep cup, and lined with hair and feathers. Outside, the bird will most likely have stuck pieces of grey or white lichen. Lichen is the papery-looking plant which grows on apple trees, and which children call grey moss. The pieces woven in help to hide the nest in an apple tree. When the Chaffinch builds in a green hedge she often uses green moss instead.

Now try to find a Thrush's nest. It may be in a laurel-bush or a fir-tree. It is large and quite firm, not soft like the hedge-sparrows nest. For the thrush plasters the inside with mud, or cow-dung, or rotten wood, till it is almost as hard as the inside of a cocoa-nut shell.

When you have looked at these nests, you will want to see one built next spring. But this is not so easy. For birds try to hide the cradles of their little ones, and do not like to work when anyone is near.

Rooks are the easiest to watch, for they build in high trees, and therefore are not shy. You may see them flying along with pieces of stick in their mouths, and bringing mud and clay to plaster them together. Sometimes you may see the old rooks staying behind in the rookery, to steal the sticks from the nests of the young rooks while they are away, instead of fetching them for themselves.

9

Birds do not all make the same shaped nests. The Lark makes her nest of grass in a rut or a furrow of the field. The green Plover or Peewit, whose cry you know so well, "pee-weet, pee-weet," lays a few bits of grass, or rush, in a marsh or in a rough field. Her little ones run about as soon as they come out of the egg.

The Swallows build their nests of mud and straw on the rafters of barns, or under the ledges of chimneys, in the shape of a shallow basin, and line them with feathers. But the Martins build under the eaves. They make their nests of clay stuck against the wall like a bag, with only a small hole at the top. It is very funny to see the tail of a martin sticking out, when she puts her head into her nest to feed the young ones.

The Woodpecker makes a hole in a tree for her nest, and lines it with chips of wood. The Nuthatch looks out for a hole in a branch, and lines it with flakes of bark and dry leaves. Then, if it is too big, she fills up the opening with clay, all except one little hole.

Rooks and Pigeons build coarse nests. The rooks build theirs of sticks and turf lined with grass and moss. The pigeon leaves hers so loose that the eggs almost slip through.

Then the little singing birds, the Warblers, the Thrushes, the Nightingales, and the Robins build lovely cup-nests. Reed-warblers weave their nest round two or three reeds, or other plants, near the water. It is made of blades of grass and lined with water-weed. The Wren, the long-tailed Titmouse, and the Chiff-chaff, build nests in the shape of a ball, with a hole in one side. The chiff-chaff lines hers with a beautifully soft layer of feathers.

Wrens build in all sorts of strange places, in walls and trees, in holes of rocks, on the tops of hedges and on the banks of rivers. If you look about near the nest in which the wren has laid her eggs you will often find one or two other nests built exactly like it, but *not lined with feathers*. They are called "cock's nests." We do not know why the birds build them. Perhaps one day you may find out if you watch. The chiff-chaff hides her nests in the hedges or banks, and the long-tailed titmouse loves to build in the gorse bushes.

REED-WARBLERS' NEST.

Once two Wrens were watched building their nest in a juniper tree. They began at seven o'clock in the morning. The mother wren brought some leaves from a lime-tree. She put one leaf in a fork of the tree, and laid the others round it. Then she went back for more. So she went on all day, bringing in leaves, and matting them together with moss, and all the while the cock-wren sang to her from the top of the tree.

By seven o'clock in the evening she had made the outside of the nest, in the shape of a ball with a hole in one side.

Next day the two birds began work together at half-past three in the morning. They worked for eight days, carrying in moss and feathers. When they had done, the nest was a firm little ball, lined with a thick layer of soft feathers, for the wee wrens to lie in, when they were hatched.

Then the mother wren laid five small white eggs with a few red spots upon them, and sat for a whole fortnight, while her mate sang to her, and brought her insects to eat.

Examine nests. Mud-built—*swallow, martin.* Roughly woven—*house-sparrow.* Cup-nests—*hedge-sparrow, chaffinch.* Woven and mud-lined—*thrush.*

CHAPTER IV: Birds' Eggs

WHEN you have looked at several birds' nests, you will want to see what the eggs are like. Try first to find those which are near your home. Some are so well hidden, that you will have to watch where the old birds go in and out, before you can find them. Others, like the nests of rooks, magpies and jays, are easy to see, but not easy to reach.

Do not take the eggs. Each will hatch out into a happy little bird, and if you carried the egg home it would only be broken. Your teacher will very likely collect one of each kind, which will do to show the class for many years.

But look well at the eggs in the nest. Then you will know them again when you find them in another place. Count how many there are, and notice if any more are laid afterwards. Then reckon how long the eggs are being hatched, after the last one is laid. You will find it is about a fortnight for the small birds and a day or two longer for rooks and pigeons. Then you can watch the feeding of the young birds, which we shall talk about in the next two lessons.

It is better not even to touch the eggs; for some birds, like the wood-pigeon, will desert their nests if the eggs have been handled. Other birds are not so particular. Mr. Kearton tells us that when he was a boy he used to find plovers' nests and amuse himself by turning the large end of the egg into the middle of the nest. As soon as the tidy mother came back, she always turned them round again with the points in the middle. The baby bird always comes out at the large end, so this gives them more room, as they hatch out.

THRUSHES AND NEST.

If you have a laurel hedge in the garden you may find a Thrush's nest in it, with four to six beautiful blue eggs, about an inch long and spotted with black at the large end. The mother will scold you well, and perhaps will not leave the nest, and you will have to take your chance when she is away. You may find a Blackbird's nest not far off. You will know it from the thrush's nest because it is lined with fine roots and grass, so is not hard inside. The eggs are greener with red-brown spots. The Misselthrush generally builds in a tree, and her eggs are a light buff colour spotted with reddish brown and pale lilac.

The Chaffinch will build close to your house, or in the apple trees of the orchard; and a pair of Bullfinches may make their nest in the ivy of the old garden wall, though they are shy birds. The chaffinch's eggs are a pale brown-green colour with brown spots. They are about one-third the size of the thrush's egg. The bullfinch's are a pale blue, spotted with brown or purple. Be careful when you look at the bullfinch's nest, for though the mother will sit still, the father will be angry, and he may make her desert her nest, if he sees you.

You will have to get a ladder if you want to see a Martin's nest, for they build under the eaves of the house. And when you pull away a little of the nest and look in, make sure that you see the right eggs, for a sparrow will often take a martin's nest and lay her eggs in it. You can find out, by watching which bird goes into the nest. But if you cannot do this, you may know by the colour of the eggs. A martin's egg is white without any spots upon it. A sparrow's egg is grey with brown blotches on it. When the sparrow builds her own nest, it is made of straw or hay lined with feathers. It has about five or six eggs in it.

It is easier to look into a Swallow's nest than into a martin's, for it is not covered at the top, and is often put upon a rafter in a barn. It will have about five white eggs in it, with dark red patches on them. Watch these nests carefully, for when the eggs are hatched it is very pretty to see the old swallows teaching the young ones to catch flies.

We must not forget the Robins, though I expect you know their eggs well. They are white, spotted with light red, and you may easily find them, for in the spring there is a robin's nest in almost every bank or hedgerow.

COCK AND HEN CHAFFINCH, WITH THEIR NEST.

You may look for a Tomtit's nest in all sorts of strange places, from a hole in a tree, to a flower-pot which has been thrown away. There will be a number of little white eggs in it speckled with red. The mother will hiss and peck at you to prevent you from taking them away. But in a few days she will not be afraid, for she is a bold little bird.

You must learn to look for other eggs yourselves. In the barn you may find the Owl's large white eggs, and sometimes young birds and eggs together. In a bank of a river, or a hole in a wall, you may find the nest of a Water-wagtail with greyish white spotted eggs. The Rook's bluish green eggs sometimes fall down from their nests; and the Jackdaws will build in your chimneys.

When you have spent some time hunting for nests and eggs, you will notice how cunningly they are hidden by their colour and their marks.

Wherever you find white eggs like those of the owl, the martin, the woodpecker, the kingfisher, and the pigeon, they are either quite hidden in a bank, a tree trunk, or a deep nest, or they are high up out of reach. Most other eggs are spotted, and they are either some shade of green or grey or brown, like the moss and leaves and twigs of the nest.

In any nest you can find, see how many of the eggs grow up into young birds. Choose one nest each, to watch and see which child can count up most young birds.

CHAPTER V: Baby Birds

THE mother bird sits on the nest and keeps the eggs warm all the time that the little birds are growing inside. She never leaves them except to stretch herself and get food. Sometimes the father bird sits while she is away, or he brings food to her. Sometimes he only sings to her.

The first thing that the baby-birds do for themselves is to get out of the egg. When they are ready you may hear them crying "cheep, cheep" inside. Then they tap away at the big end with a little horny tip, which grows on the top of their beak, and the shell cracks, and out they come.

If you can catch a chicken as soon as it is out of the egg, you may see this horny tip. But you must be quick, for a chicken is a very active baby-bird. It runs about directly it is hatched, and the horny tip falls off.

The next thing young birds do is to open their beaks and cry for food. Some, like the chickens, ducks, and partridges come out with downy feathers all over them. These run about and get food for themselves. Their mother takes care of them, and they cuddle under her wing when she calls to them.

Others, like the pigeon, the sparrow, and the thrush, are naked, blind, and helpless when they are hatched. They cannot get out of the nest, and their parents have to feed them.

If you keep doves in a cage, or if you can climb up to the pigeon-boxes where the pigeons have their nests, you may learn a good deal by watching a baby pigeon.

The day it comes out of the egg its eyelids are tightly closed. It has only a few downy tufts on its naked body, so you can see its fleshy wing and feel the bones. Handle it carefully and notice that its wing has three joints, just like your arm. One at the *shoulder (s)* close to the body, one at the *elbow (e)*, and one at the *wrist (w)*.

18

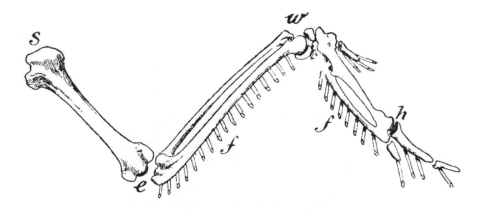

BONES OF A BIRD'S WING. (S) SHOULDER. (E) ELBOW. (W) WRIST. (H) HAND. (F) FEATHER QUILLS.

As it lies in the nest, it draws its elbow back and touches its shoulder with its hand. Then the wing is shut. But if you take hold of the hand *(h)* gently, and pull the arm out straight, then the wing is open. This is just what a bird does when he stretches his wings to fly.

Now watch the little ones day by day. By degrees pimples come out all over the body. Then the middle of each pimple sinks in and some feathers peep out. The first feathers are quite limp. The little featherlets grow all round the stem like hairs on a cat's tail. These are the down feathers. There are not many on a young pigeon.

The next feathers are quite different. They are flat and much stiffer. The featherlets only grow on each side of the stem. They are tinted, and you can see now whether the pigeon is going to be white or coloured.

It is these "covering" feathers which are so beautiful in most birds. They do not grow all over the body. If you push back the feathers of a dead bird you will see that they grow in places only, and spread themselves over the rest.

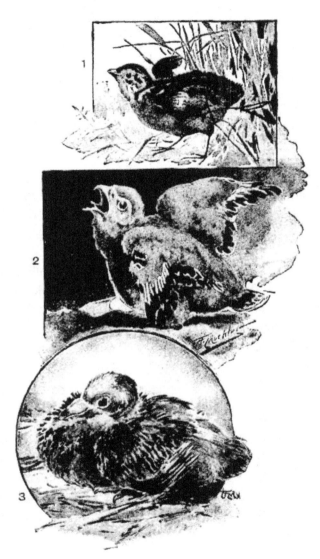

BABY BIRDS— 1. PARTRIDGE 2. KESTREL 3. PIGEON

Meanwhile the long tail and wing feathers have been growing. Those for the tip of the wing grow on the *hand*, those for the edge of the wing on the *arm*, between the wrist and the elbow, and above these, like tiles on a roof, grow the small feathers right up to the *shoulder*, making the wing round and firm.

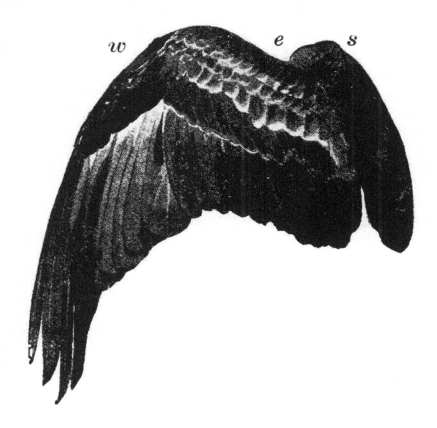

A FEATHERED WING. (S) SHOULDER. (E) ELBOW. (W) WRIST.

Feel one of the long wing feathers. It has a strong quill down the middle, which tapers away at the end so that the feather will bend, Now try to pull the featherlets apart. You will find that they stick together, as if they were glued. This is because there are tiny hooks all along each little branch, by which it is hooked on to the next one. So when the wings beat the air, it cannot pass through them, especially as the small side of each feather lies over the broad side of the next one.

By this time the young pigeons will have opened their eyes. But though they can stand up, they are very weak, and take all their food from their mother.

Then about a month after coming out of the egg, they go to the edge of the pigeon-house and watch the other pigeons. From time to time they stretch out their wings, and flap them a little. As they flap them downwards, the air under the front of the wing cannot get away there, and is driven out behind just as water is driven by an oar when we row. But as they lift the wing up again the feathers turn so that the air can pass through. Therefore, as they flap their wings they raise themselves a little, and flutter to the next ledge, and at last they fly to the ground and begin to pick up food with their parents.

Compare a young pigeon and a young chicken. Examine the down feathers, covering feathers, and long quill feathers.

CHAPTER VI: Birds Feeding Their Young

YOU will find it very interesting to peep into nests and see which birds are naked and which are downy, which can see, and which are blind.

By the river the little Water-hens come out of the egg as black fluffy balls with red heads, and swim away at once after their mother. But Kingfishers come out of the egg naked and helpless. They have to wait till their feathers have grown, before they can leave the nest, and meanwhile their mother feeds them with fish.

Then if you see a young Owl in its nest in a barn, or pick up a young Hawk which has fallen out of a tree, you will find that they are quite blind and helpless, though they are covered with down. Their mothers have to bring them insects, mice, and young rabbits till they are full-grown.

Those of you who live by the seaside know quite well the Gulls which fly out to sea and float on the waves. In the spring and early summer you may hear the young gulls, called Sea-mews or Kittiwakes, mewing like kittens on the ledges of the cliffs. They are calling to their parents to feed them.

For though these young gulls can see and are covered with down, they are born so high up on the cliffs that they must sit and wait till they are strong. Even then they can only creep along the ledges till their wings are full-grown. They sit there with open beaks, crying to be fed, and the old sea-birds bring fish for them to eat. The common gulls, and the herring gulls, generally lay their eggs on islands, and the little ones swim about when they are only a few days old.

Or, if you live far away from the sea in the depths of the country, you will enjoy seeing the other kinds of birds feeding their young ones in the trees and in the hedges. Sometimes the mother does all the work, and sometimes the father takes his share.

SEA GULLS AND YOUNG.

OWL FEEDING HER LITTLE ONES.

25

Birds of the Air

Mr. Kearton, who knows so much about birds, tells us that he once helped in the feeding. One day he watched a mother Chiff-chaff bringing food to her five little ones in a nest under a thorn-bush. Chiff-chaffs are very small, graceful birds. Their back and wings are a kind of dull olive green colour, and their breast a yellowish white. The mother was bringing in caterpillars and flies, about four or five every five minutes, and she popped them into the little beaks stretched to reach them. As she worked, her mate flew first to one bough, then to another singing "chiff-chaff, chiff-chaff."

Mr. Kearton thought he would help the little mother. He collected some green caterpillars, and put them on the edge of the nest while she was away. Then he knelt down a little way off.

The mother flew to and fro at her work and looked at him as she passed, but he did not move. At last she picked up the insects he had brought and divided them among the little mouths. Then she flew away for more.

That little mother worked all day long, only resting for half an hour in the afternoon. She not only brought food, but also cleaned the nest between each journey, picking out the pellets of dung, and making everything clean and neat. I think she must have been very glad of the little heaps of insects which her friend put near her nest from time to time.

Tomtits are such bold little birds that you may often see them going in and out of a hole in some wall, or a tree stump, with insects in their mouths. The father and mother Tit both help in feeding. They go out and come back together, laden with caterpillars, and after giving them to the young ones they start off again, calling to each other as they go.

We had some young Robins once which were fed by three birds. They were born in the hedge of our garden. We called the third bird the uncle. He worked quite as hard as the other two. By-and-bye the old robins flew away. But the young ones stayed with us all the summer and used to hop about the dinner table and pick up the crumbs.

Blackbirds feed their baby-birds with large worms, which they pull to pieces, giving a bit to each. The jay looks as if she brought nothing, but she pours the food from her crop into the mouth of the little one. The mother pigeon throws the food up from her crop into her mouth, and the little pigeon puts its beak in at the side of its mother's beak and sucks out the food.

Most parent birds go on feeding the little ones for some time after they can fly. You may often see little sparrows or thrushes sitting in a row on a bough while the mother pops the food into their beaks. She begins at one end and goes quite fairly from one to another, each in its turn.

Watch for birds feeding young in the spring. Thrushes, sparrows, robins, tomtits. 1. In the nest. 2. Sitting on branches. 3. Small birds feeding a young cuckoo. 4. Young pigeon taking food from the mother.

CHAPTER VII: Where Do Birds Sleep?

WHERE are all the birds at night? In the daytime we see them in the fields, on the trees and hedges, or on the cliffs. They feed in the garden, the orchard, and the wood. But in the evening, when the sun sets, we hear them singing as if they were saying "good-night," and then they disappear. Only the night birds are about after sunset. Owls hoot and fly after dark, nightingales sing all night in warm summer weather, and if there are any corn-crakes about, you will hear their tiresome cry, "craake, craake," long after you want to go to sleep.

But the other birds are nowhere to be seen. Where are they? It is not easy to find them, for they hide themselves, from fear of the owls, the weasels and the stoats, and they wake and flutter away very soon if you come near them.

The small birds sleep chiefly in the hedges. You will be surprised how difficult it is to see them, even in winter when the leaves are off the trees; for the twigs and branches crossing each other hide them well. No owl or hawk could seize a bird in a hawthorn hedge.

But how do they keep themselves upon the twigs when they are fast asleep? If you or I tried to sleep standing up we should fall. For our muscles would grow slack, our heads would nod, and our knees would give way under us.

It is different with a bird. He sits on a branch, and grasps it with his claws. Then he squats down and bends his legs. As he does this, a muscle round his knee-joints pulls the muscles of his toes quite tight, so that his claws are kept clasped round the branch. He cannot move till he has raised himself up and straightened his legs, and thus set his claws free. So the more soundly he sleeps the tighter he grasps the bough, and the less likely he is to fall.

Birds sleep out of doors both summer and winter, and they have a curious covering to keep them warm. It is made of air. When a bird goes to roost, he tucks his head under the plumage of his shoulder, and puffs out his feathers, so that the air gets in between them, and settles all among the soft down which grows close to his body. This air soon becomes warm, and, as it cannot get out, it prevents the bird's warm body from being chilled by the cold air outside.

Still, in bad weather birds often like to find warm nooks to sleep in. House-sparrows, tits, wrens, and other small birds sometimes make holes in hay-stacks for their beds. The owls keep themselves warm in barns, church towers, and sometimes in holes in the trunks of trees. The blue-tit loves to sleep under a thatched roof, and Wrens often hunt up old nests in winter, and huddle together in them to keep themselves warm.

Swallows and swifts do not want to be kept warm, for they fly south in cold weather. In summer they perch on the rafters in the barns, and if you go into a barn after dark, you may often hear them flitting from one rafter to another if they are disturbed.

Wood-pigeons roost on the fir-trees in the wood, and hawks on the branches of the taller trees. Pheasants, too, roost in the trees of the wood, and it is curious that they always tell you where they go to bed. For they call "crok, crok," as they settle down to sleep.

But partridges sleep on the ground in the fields. They lie in a circle with their heads outwards and their tails together. The father generally sleeps a little way off as a sentinel. Then if a fox, or a weasel, tries to catch them in their sleep, any one that is awake and sees the enemy can give the alarm to the rest.

BLUE TITS AND YOUNG.

All these birds sleep inland in the woods and fields. But if you can go to the sea-shore some summer evening and lie on the beach under the high cliffs, you may see other birds coming home to roost. Just as the sun is setting many little birds from the fields perch in the bushes at the top of the rocks. Next come any jackdaws, which happen to live near the sea, cackling and chasing each other over the cliffs. They creep into holes to sleep. Then a few big cormorants sail in from the sea, followed by the gulls, and settle on the ledges half-way down the face of the cliff. Some croaking ravens come flying from the land, and twist and tumble about, before they too sit down for the night. The sand-martins disappear into their holes in the sandstone-rocks, and perhaps a falcon will come circling round in the air and swoop down in some quiet nook.

CORMORANTS FEEDING.

Then after a time the cackling and the croaking cease and as the moon rises all is quiet. But if you look on the silvery water you will see that many of

31

the gulls are still floating on the waves, and they may remain there all the night.

Watch the birds going to roost at night, and notice their special haunts.

CHAPTER VIII: Feeding in Summer

SPRING and summer are happy times for birds. Then there is plenty of food for them and their little ones. Let us go out some fine summer morning, and watch the different birds as they feed. You will not see them all in one day. But you ought to find each one some time during the summer.

Close to the house you are sure to see a House Sparrow picking up scraps in the yard and eating the caterpillars and red spiders on the gooseberry bushes in the kitchen garden. For the sparrow is not dainty. He will eat most things, from a grain of wheat to a scrap of meat.

In the kitchen garden, too, you may see the Chaffinch breaking the husks of seeds with his sharp little beak. He is not particular whether he takes them from the weeds, or from the beds of radishes or turnips which we have sown. But he does us more good than harm, for he destroys a great deal of groundsel and chickweed.

Out in the fields the little brown Lark, which has been singing in the sky, drops down to hunt for seeds in the furrows turned up by the plough. In the rickyard I can see several little Finches, the greenfinch and the yellowhammer, picking up the grains of corn.

All these birds feed usually on grain, and have short sharp beaks which will split the husks, though they sometimes eat insects and feed their young ones on them. We have to drive them away from our wheat and oats for a few weeks in the year, but they are very useful in keeping down the weeds, for they eat every seed they can find.

The Swallows, Swifts, and Martins have very different beaks. If you watch them as they skim along in the air, you will see they can open their mouths very wide to catch the flies and gnats. But the hard beak itself is very small. They have weak legs and strong wings, for they catch all their food as they fly. Notice how near the ground they keep in dull weather. Then the insects are flying low, and the swallows follow them. But on a bright day the gnats and midges fly higher, so swallows fly higher too.

1. BULLFINCH (GRAIN-FEEDER) 2. SWALLOW (FLY-FEEDER) 3. LINNET 4. LARK (BOTH GRAIN- AND INSECT-FEEDERS).

That big Thrush which is hopping about on the grass is very different from the swallows. He has strong feet and legs, and a long, narrow, round beak. He feeds on worms and snails in the summer, and on berries in the autumn. Look at him now. He has his feet firmly planted on the grass, and he is pulling away at a worm with all his might. He will get it out of the ground soon, and carry it away to feed his little ones.

Many of the smaller perching birds feed only on insects. I am sure you will love them. They are such pretty little things. First, there is the Wagtail with his black and white wings, and his long tail bobbing up and down as he hunts for insects in the grass. Not far off is a little Wren hopping on a rose-tree and picking off the green-fly, which does so much harm.

On a bush near, sits a small brown bird with a grey speckled breast. He only came back to England from warm countries at the end of May. He is the common spotted Fly-catcher. Look how still he sits. Then all at once he darts into the air with wide open mouth, snaps his beak, and goes back to his place. He has caught a fly and will now sit and wait for another.

SPOTTED FLY-CATCHER.

Next I want you to look at a little bird which I love because he is so bright and gay. He is a Blue Tit or Tomtit, a small bird with a bright blue head and wings, and a yellow breast. He is hanging upside down on the branch of a tree watching for spiders. When he has caught one he will flutter off to another tree and get a good breakfast in a very little while. He is a very bold little bird, and in the winter you may learn to know him well, if you will give him some food.

These birds, the thrush, the wagtail, the flycatcher, the wren and the tomtit are very useful to us. They kill the snails and slugs, the caterpillars, maggots, and grubs. So do the nightingale and the blackbird, and another little bird, which I want you to know. This is the Hedge-sparrow, a small brown bird with a blue-grey breast, which flutters along the lanes. I am sure you must have seen him. He picks up a tiny insect, flits a little way and picks up another, and then flits away again just in front of you as you walk along the lane. You must not confuse him with the house-sparrow. He is quite another kind of bird, he is one of the warblers and sings very sweetly. He is sometimes called the "hedge-warbler," and this is a much better and truer name for him.

We have not much time to watch other birds, But we must look at the rooks hunting for worms and slugs in the ploughed fields; and as we come near the wood I see a partridge feeding on ants under the trees. He flies away with a loud whirr long before we get near him, and as he cries "cluck, cluck" I expect the mother bird and her nest are not far off.

If you go into the wood you may see the little Tree-creeper running up the trees looking for insects, and the woodpecker darting out his sticky tongue and tapping at the trunks of the trees, and the wood-pigeon flying home with her crop full of oats or peas to feed her little ones.

Or if you stroll by the river there may be the tiny kingfisher darting down to seize tiny fish; or the grave heron sitting quite still, with his neck stretched out, till in a moment his head shoots forward, and he brings up a big eel in his beak.

You can notice many of these things for yourselves. The great secret is to look at every bird you see and try to learn something about it.

Notice the hard beaks of birds which eat seeds—Chaffinch. The hooked beaks of birds which eat flesh—Hawk. The wide gape of birds which catch insects on the wing—Swallow. The long, slender beaks of birds which feel underground for food—Woodcock.

CHAPTER IX: Migrating in Autumn

WHEN the summer is over, there is not so much food for the birds, and some begin to go away. Those which live on flying insects go first. The cuckoo is generally gone by the end of July. The swifts start off in August, and about the middle of September the swallows begin to find very few flies, gnats, or moths, and get ready for their long journey.

If you keep a sharp look-out you may see the Swallows and Martins collecting, about the 15th of September, on some church tower, or perhaps on the roof of a barn, and flying off together to roost in the trees. This they never do in the summer. Then they sleep on the rafters of some barn, or under the eaves of a roof, always keeping near buildings. But before they fly away for the winter they gather together in the trees, or on the willows in the osier beds.

Then some morning very early they all disappear. They have started to fly steadily in large flocks, for hundreds of miles, to Africa, where they will have warm weather, and insects to eat, all the winter. You will not see them again till next April.

The little Fly-catchers and the Nightingales go away about the same time as the swallows, and the Chiff-chaff goes in October. Some of the Wagtails and Robins go too, but not nearly all.

MARTIN; AND SWALLOW FEEDING HER YOUNG.

FLIGHT OF SWALLOWS.

A great many birds shift from place to place in England during the autumn, for food begins to be scarce, and they wander in search of it. Many thrushes and redwings come to us from Norway and Germany, and robins, finches, and other birds come from the north of England to the south. They leave the cold moors and mountains of Cumberland and Yorkshire to feed in Hampshire and Devonshire, where they can find more berries, such as hips and haws, holly-berries, juniper-berries, sloes, and the red berries of the mountain ash. So if you live in the south of England, you may see more robins, thrushes, chaffinches, and yellow-hammers in the winter than you did in the summer.

You will find it very interesting to watch for the different birds, and see when they come and go, and whether you see many or few of any one kind.

You will notice that in winter the little birds move about in flocks, instead of alone, or in pairs, as they do in the summer, when they have their nests and families. In November you will see a great many larks together. The cock-chaffinches sometimes fly in one flock, and the hen-chaffinches in another. The Finches, too, fly in parties; yellow-hammers, greenfinches, and goldfinches all together. They hunt about for seeds, and sleep on the ground, or in the ivy bushes. But the Bullfinches, with their lovely blue-black wings and bright red breasts, keep together in small flocks, flying in a line one after the other along the hedges.

These flocks of different birds flit about from one field to another, keeping together, and scattering over one place at a time, looking for food.

When many of our summer birds have gone to the sunny south, other birds come to us from still colder countries. The Fieldfares fly over from Norway and Sweden. You may see them, in parties of about forty or fifty, wheeling round in the air, and settling down on a field to look for grubs and seeds. They are pretty grey birds with brown-red wings and buff speckled breasts. But you cannot often get near enough to see them, for they are very shy. If they hear a noise they are off in a moment, and over the hedge into the next field, where they drop down again to feed. They sleep on the ground; and go back to Norway to build their nests in the spring.

A great many Starlings come from Norway and Germany in the winter, and join those which live with us always. They often fly about with the rooks, but sometimes in flocks by themselves pecking in the fields and chattering one to another.

So when the song-birds are silent in the winter, you can look out for all these other birds and find out where they feed and sleep; when you first see them come, and when you see the last one go. But the thrush and the robin will sing all the year through, when the weather is mild.

Make a list of summer birds which you do not see in the winter. Make a list of winter birds which go away in the spring. Make another list of birds you see all the year round.

CHAPTER X: Bird-Food in Winter

WHEN Christmas is past and the real winter cold begins, the poor little birds often have a hard time. So long as the weather is mild, the thrush picks out the slugs and snails from their hiding-places in the walls and palings. The robin and the wren bustle about, looking for seeds and insects. The little wagtails run about the lawns wagging their tails, as they try to find a stray grub, or beetle. In the wood the tree-creeper hunts for spiders and the eggs of insects in the bark of the trees, and the nut-hatches and pigeons feed under the beeches.

But after a while, when a hard frost comes, and snow lies deep on the ground, the birds look very sad. The larks and the linnets crouch down under the banks of the cornfields to keep warm. The thrushes fly from tree to tree to look for a few mistletoe berries, now that all the others are eaten. The chaffinches and the yellow-hammers fly round the farmer's ricks, to pull out some grains of wheat or oats, or grass seeds. The fieldfares wander sadly about in flocks. The rooks, starlings, and jackdaws fly from field to field screaming and cawing as they try to find some place where the wind has blown the snow away and they can peck in the furrows. The lapwings, which you may know by the feathers which stand up on the back of their head, cry "peewit, peewit" mournfully, as they journey to the sea-coast, where they find food on the sands and mudflats at low tide.

STARLINGS IN WINTER.

It is sad to think how often little birds are starved to death. They do not so much mind the cold, for you remember that the air under their feathers keeps them warm. But in a hard winter they often die from want of food. If you pick up a dead robin, starling, or rook after a long frost, you will find that the bones are only covered with skin and feathers. Its flesh has all wasted away.

Now is your time to be kind to the birds which have sung to you all the summer. They did good work then, eating the caterpillars and grubs, the wire-worms and maggots, the slugs and snails, and keeping down the weeds by eating the seeds. Now you can feed them, for a little while, till the frost and snow are gone.

You will learn to know a great many birds in this way, and you need only give them a few scraps, which you can well spare. Some birds, you will remember, like seeds and crumbs and green food. Others, which eat insects in the summer, will be glad of a little gristle or fat.

So you must save up every scrap from breakfast, dinner, and supper, and keep it for the next morning—crusts of bread, the crumbs off the table, cold potatoes, and potato skins. You can get your mother to boil the potatoes in their skins, and then the birds will like the peel. Perhaps, too, you may save some pieces of cabbage, some apple parings, and a little fat.

All this will make a nice dish for starving birds, if you chop it up and pour a little hot water over the crusts. And if you live on a farm you may be able to sweep up a few grains of corn in the stables, before they are thrown away with the manure.

Then clear the snow away in front of your door, throw the food down and go back out of sight. The birds will soon come, and in a few days they will even be waiting about for their morning meal before you bring it.

You must not forget to hang a piece of fat from the branch of a tree, so that you may see the tits hang head downwards on the string to peck at it. And if you hang up a bone with a little meat on it the starlings and jackdaws will come too.

Then remember that birds want to drink. You can put water for them in a pan, if you change it when it freezes. But if you can spare a few pence to buy a cocoa-nut, you may make it serve two purposes.

BIRDS FEEDING IN WINTER.

Saw it across the middle, and scoop out all the white from one half. Bore two holes near the rim of this cup, and make a handle with a piece of string. Then hang it on a tree and put some water in it. The birds will sit on the rim and drink. And as they make it swing to and fro the water will not freeze. Then hang up the other half in the same way, but leave the white inside. The little tomtits will peck away, and fight for the sweet food till it is all gone.

A number of birds will come—robins, chaffinches, sparrows, wrens, starlings, rooks, jackdaws, thrushes, and many others. You will be able to notice the difference between the big missel-thrush, with his white spotted breast, and the smaller brown song-thrush. And if you put some nuts on the window-sill the nuthatch may come to fetch them if he lives near.

So you will see the birds more closely than you can at any other time, and next summer, when they sing in the trees, they will be old friends.

Make a list of the birds which come to feed at your door in winter.

CHAPTER XI: Other Small Birds

THERE are many other small birds which you may find out for yourselves, but I should like to tell you of a few which are interesting. First there is the little Goldfinch, which is so useful to us because it eats thistle seeds and dandelion seeds. It builds a lovely little nest of fine roots, wool, and horsehair, and often lines it with the soft down of the coltsfoot, that big yellow flower which blooms in the spring and has feathery seed-boxes. The goldfinch has a beautiful red forehead and throat, and black wings barred with yellow, and tipped with white. You may know it from the bullfinch because its breast is pale brown, while the bullfinch has a rich red breast and grey and black wings.

Then there is the cock-Linnet with his crimson breast, brown wings, and a red patch on his head. Linnets change colour at different times of the year. In the winter, the breasts of both birds are grey striped with brown.

All birds *moult,* that is change their feathers, at least once a year. The father-birds are nearly always more gaudy when they are building their nests. You will notice too that hen-birds are scarcely ever so gay as their mates. This is most likely because they sit on the nests, and it would not do for them to be seen too easily.

Linnets feed in big flocks in the winter. You may see them in the evening dropping down among the gorse and other bushes to sleep. It is sad that both the goldfinch and the linnet are caught and sold to sing in cages. This is why we have not nearly so many in England as we used to have.

I hope you will look out for the Nuthatch, a little bird with a short black beak, a blue-grey back and wings, and a pale yellow breast, shaded with red. He is often seen in orchards and gardens in the autumn, when the nuts are ripe. You may catch sight of him coming down a nut tree, head downwards. He sticks the nuts into the cracks of the trunk and hammers

47

them with his beak to break them. You may sometimes find a little store of nuts which he has hidden at the foot of the tree. He feeds on other things, besides nuts and beech-mast, and he will peck at a piece of bacon in winter, if you hang it out for him.

You must listen for the Blackcap. You will hear him more easily than you will see him. He is a little dark grey bird, with a black head and a pale grey breast, and sings almost as well as a nightingale. He comes back to England in April, and if you listen well you may hear him practising his song. He hides himself in a thick bush and begins gently in a low voice, singing over and over again till he gains strength. In a few days his voice is ready, and he trills out a wild, sweet song all the summer day, flitting from bush to bush as he sings. He feeds on insects and berries, and brings up four or five little ones in a lovely nest made of dry grass and spiders' webs, and lined with horsehair. Then he flies away in October till the next spring. But he has been so often caught that he is not so common as he used to be.

Then there is the little Whitethroat, which creeps along almost everywhere under the hedges, and is often called the "nettle-creeper." He too is a brown-grey bird with a little red at the tips of his feathers and on his breast. He hops and flies a little way as the hedge-sparrow does, chattering all the time, and sometimes flying higher and higher and singing louder. He, too, comes in May and goes in October.

There are two other little birds you may very likely see. One is the Stonechat, which lives on commons and sits on the top of the furze bushes. It is a small brown-black bird with white markings and a rusty red breast. It cries "chat, chat, chat," and hides its nest so well in the gorse bushes that you will scarcely find one.

The other is the little Dipper or water-ouzel, which hops about the stones in the bed of rapid streams and rivers. It feeds on insects and water snails. It is a black bird not quite as big as a thrush, with a very short tail and a snowy-white breast. It has a curious way of dipping its head down and flirting its tail.

There is not room to tell about magpies or jays, but if you have any near you, you will know them already.

Find out these small birds and any others in your neighbourhood, and try to know their nests and eggs.

BLACK-CAPS IN A MAPLE BUSH.

CHAPTER XII: Birds of Prey

WE call "Birds of Prey" those which feed on the smaller animals, such as rabbits, mice, frogs, and snakes, as well as on other birds. The chief kinds in our country are eagles, falcons, hawks, and owls.

If you live in the mountains of Scotland, or the north of England, you may, perhaps, have seen an eagle. But the birds of prey you are most likely to know are hawks and owls.

I am sure that sometimes when you are in the fields, you must have seen a bird with long pointed wings and a tail like a fan hovering in the air. This is the Kestrel or common hawk. Country people call him the "wind-hover." His wings beat the air so quickly that you can scarcely see them move, yet he keeps quite still in the same place. His bright eyes look eagerly on the ground. Now he darts a little up or down, and floats along some distance. Now he hovers again, and all at once drops to the ground. He has seen a mouse in the grass, and rises up with it in his claws.

Farmers often shoot kestrels because they steal young partridges and chickens, when they cannot find other food. But they are very useful in killing field-mice, moles, beetles, and all kinds of vermin.

If you cannot tame a young hawk, nor find a dead one, you can see on pp. 51 and 61 how to know a bird of prey. Look at the long toes and sharp claws of the eagle or the hawk. They pierce the skin of any animal he seizes. His hooked beak is very strong, and has sharp edges, so that it cuts like shears. The upper half is pointed, and hangs over the lower half. A few strong pecks with this cruel beak soon kill the tiny mouse or larger animals, which are swallowed whole or torn to pieces. After a little time the furry skins and the bones are thrown up in a ball. The feet and legs of a bird of prey are covered with scales, so that when he is fighting he is not so much hurt by hard pecks.

GOLDEN EAGLE.

BARN OWL AND KESTREL HAWK.

The kestrel's wings are strong and pointed, and he can fly quickly, or keep himself floating, as he pleases. He is about as large as a wood-pigeon. His back and wings are a bright brick-red, and his tail is grey, tipped with white, with a black band across. The long feathers of his wings are black, while his breast is pale yellow.

Another common hawk is the Sparrow-hawk, which has dark grey wings and a reddish-brown breast with orange stripes. He does not often hover, but glides along the hedges looking for birds and mice. He does more harm than the kestrel, for he often kills game. But he is useful in destroying mice, and insects, and in preventing the small birds, which eat the corn, from becoming too numerous. The mother sparrow-hawk is much larger than the father.

Owls, like hawks, have hooked beaks and long sharp claws. But their beak is not so strong, and their feet are more useful for climbing. Their four toes stand, three in front and one behind, like most birds, but they can turn back the outer front toe so as to have two in front and two behind, like the woodpecker.

Notice too the difference in their eyes. A hawk has his eyes on the sides of his head, but the owl has his in front of his face like you or I. So, when he hunts in the twilight, he can peer down at things close to him. He can make the pupil of his eye as large as the cat does, so as to gather all the light there is. His feathers are so soft and downy that he makes very little noise as he flies, and he has large hidden ears with flaps over them, and can hear the slightest sound. Some owls have ear tufts sticking up in the air like a cat's ear.

The owl you hear so often crying "to-whoo, to-whoo" is the brown or Tawny Owl. He hunts in the early morning and late evening. In the day-time he hides in holes of the trees and in church towers. If he is driven into the sunlight he winks and blinks, and cannot see clearly. But in the dusk, or the moonlight he flies noiselessly along the hedges, and catches mice, moles, frogs, and birds, swallowing the small ones whole and throwing back the feathers and skin in little balls.

The Barn Owl is a much lighter bird than the brown owl. His back and wings are buff colour and his breast and face are white. He cries "te-whit, te-whee" in a loud screech, and is therefore often called the "Screech Owl." He hides in the barn, or in trees, by day and hunts by night, feeding chiefly on mice. When he comes out by daylight the chaffinches and other little birds tease him, for they know he cannot see well.

Compare a hawk and an owl. Notice the cere, or piece of bare skin at the top of the beak, which all birds of prey have. It is partly covered by bristles in the owls. Try to draw the foot and beak of the eagle, pp. 51 and 73.

CHAPTER XIII: Rooks and Their Companions

"YOU go and scare they rooks out o' that field. They be eating all the seed," I heard a Devonshire farmer say to his boy one day. He was quite right. He had not sown his wheat deep enough, and the rooks were feeding on it.

But some time after another farmer pointed to the rooks in his field, where the corn was green. "See how they be pulling up they young oats," said he. And so they were. But when we looked at the plants which they had pecked up, we found that each one had a place in the root where a grub had been living.

This time the rooks had been doing useful work. Wire-worms and other grubs eat away the roots of grass, corn, and turnips all across a field. When the rooks kill a few grubs, they often save the whole crop.

Once, a long time ago, some Devonshire farmers gave a large reward for rooks' heads, thinking they did harm to the farms. All the rooks around were soon killed. But the farmers were sorry afterwards. During the next three years all their crops were destroyed by insects and grubs. They had to persuade some fresh rooks to build in their neighbourhood to keep down the insects.

No doubt rooks do some mischief, for they eat birds' eggs, and newly sown corn, new potatoes, and green walnuts. They even sometimes pull grain out of the stacks, when they are short of food. But they destroy so many wire-worms and grubs, snails and slugs, maggots and insects of all kinds, that they do more good than harm.

You all know the heavy whirring cockchafer, which flops into your face in the evening. But perhaps you do not know that before he had wings he lived for three or four years underground feeding on the roots of grass and corn. Rooks eat these cockchafer grubs wherever they can find them, and so save our crops.

I hope you have rooks near you, for they are delightful to watch. When they build their huge nests high up in the forks of trees, they make a great deal of noise and bustle. The father-rook begins to fetch food for his mate even before she lays her eggs, and feeds her all the time she is sitting.

The old birds feed the young ones long after they are hatched. If you watch, you may see the young ones sitting on the edge of the nest opening their mouths to be fed. Rooks like to build near old houses, and use the same nests year after year. They will not allow strange rooks to join them.

If the trees in which they build lose their leaves in winter, the rooks do not stay there long after the last young ones are able to fly. About August or September they often go to the beech and pine woods to sleep, and do not come back to their rookery till the spring. But every now and then on their way to and fro they call at their rookery and look after their nests.

Crows do not live together in numbers like rooks. They live in pairs, and build their nests in the top of some high tree away from houses. They are more mischievous than rooks, for they feed on birds and young lambs, young pigeons, ducks, or chickens.

You may tell a crow from a rook at a distance because you very seldom see more than two together. When you can see them near, you will know them apart, because the rook, after he is a year old, has a bald patch on his head just above his beak, where the crow has feathers.

Have you ever noticed how gravely a rook walks across a field? He does not hop like a thrush or a sparrow, but moves one foot after the other, and gives a little jump every now and then. One or two always remain on the trees near, to give notice of danger, and when these sentinels cry "caw-caw" the whole flock rises. They fly away, flapping their wings slowly, and drop down one by one in another field.

A friend of mine who lives near a rookery says she often sees from her window one or two sentinel rooks go round every morning and wake up the others, and it is very funny to see how the lazy ones scramble up in a great hurry at the last, so as to be in time to fly away with the rest.

Though rooks will not allow another party of their own kind to join them, they allow starlings, jackdaws, and fieldfares to feed with them. A Jackdaw moves much like a rook, though he is a more sprightly bird. He is smaller and has a grey patch on his head. The Starling is a walking bird. Though his head and back are black, he has so many bright colours on the tips of his feathers that he does not look so dark as the rook and the jackdaw, but very bright and gay.

ROOKS IN A ROOKERY.

JACKDAWS.

I wonder why these birds like so much to follow the rooks? Perhaps it is because the rook has a keen scent, and turns up the earth for food with his long beak. The jackdaw and starling only pick up what they find above ground, so when the rook turns up the earth, they may get some of the food.

Try to see a rook, a crow, a jackdaw, and a starling, a magpie and a jay, and point out how you know them apart.

CHAPTER XIV: Web-Footed Birds

BESIDES the birds which live and feed on the land there are a great many which live mostly on the water. Some of these are called "waders," and some are "swimmers" and have webbed feet. We read about two waders, the coot and the moorhen, in Book II. To-day we will talk about the swimming birds.

If you live by the seaside, you will know the gulls which float on the sea, and often fly a long way up the rivers. Gulls come up the river Thames as far as London, and feed in the ponds of the parks. In the winter it is a pretty sight to watch them circling round and round, and catching the food which people throw to them.

You may have seen Cormorants, big black birds which fly heavily over the sea, with their long necks stretched out and their narrow wings beating the air. Then they settle on the water, and suddenly jump up and dive down head foremost, presently coming up with a fish, which it takes them often some time to swallow.

But if you live in the country near a large lake or a river, you are more likely to see a curious little swimming bird called the little Grebe or dabchick. This is a brown bird with a thin neck and head, which paddles about among the reeds on the bank of a river, or swims along quietly, diving down every now and then to catch water-snails, fish, or weeds. You will have to move very quietly if you want to get near the dabchick, for it dives down at the least alarm and comes up a long way off, out of sight.

If you have not seen any of these web-footed birds, nor even a wild duck yet every child knows the tame Duck which lives in our farmyards. Our ducks and drakes were tamed long, long ago from wild ducks, and are still very like them. Let us see what we can learn about a duck.

First I want you to look at her as she waddles across the yard. Her feet have a skin between the three front toes which joins them together. That is to say she is "web-footed." Now notice that, as she lifts her foot, the skin folds up like a fan, and when she puts her foot down, it spreads out again. When she reaches the pond, she glides into the water and begins to paddle, using one foot after the other, just as you do when you walk. In clear water you can see that as she puts her foot forward the skin shuts up, as it did when she walked, but when she puts it back and strikes the water, it opens and makes a paddle, and so she rows herself along.

FEET OF BIRDS. 1. BIRD OF PREY—EAGLE. 2. WEB-FOOTED— GOOSE. 3. SCRATCHING—PHEASANT. 4. CLIMBING— WOODPECKER. 5&6. PERCHING—MISSEL-THRUSH AND LARK.

Her legs grow far back on her body, so that she can use them to twist and turn herself about, and she can tip her head and body down into the water to look for water-snails and tadpoles, while she paddles along with her tail up in the air.

Next notice how light her body is. It floats quite on the top of the water. This is partly because she has a layer of light fat under her skin, and

61

partly because she has a thick covering of down under her feathers. There is a great deal of air caught in this down, and this makes her light.

Do you know why her feathers do not get wet and draggled in the water? The reason is very curious. Her outer feathers are all smeared with oil which she gets from a little pocket near her tail. Look at her when she comes out of the water. She presses her beak against her tail and then draws the feathers through the beak. When she has oiled them in this way, they are water-proof and keep the wet off her body.

Next watch her as she feeds. She goes gobble, gobble through the mud, and often throws her head up to swallow something she has found. Her beak is broad and flat. It is hooked at the tip, but higher up it is covered with a soft skin full of nerves. With this skin the duck feels what is in the mud as well as if she saw it. The tip and edges of the beak are very horny and sharp, and, both above and below, it is lined with thin strips of horn. When she closes her beak these strips fit into each other and make a strainer. With her sharp beak she cuts the weeds or kills the snails. With the strainer she sifts the mud and keeps the food in her mouth, forcing out the water with her thick tongue. Geese, swans, and all wild ducks have feet and beaks much like our farmyard duck.

(A) DUCK'S HEAD. (B) BILL SHOWING THE EDGES OF THE STRAINER

You may have seen wild-ducks in the lakes or rivers. The drake is a very handsome bird. His head and neck are a dark shiny green. He has a white collar, and his breast is the colour of a chestnut. His wings and back are partly brown and partly green. The four middle feathers of his tail are a glossy black and curl up. The others are grey, edged with white. When the wild drake changes his coat in June he puts off this beautiful plumage, and puts on a plain brown and grey suit, like the mother duck, till August. Then he begins to moult again, and in October is as gay as before.

The cormorants and gulls have not beaks like the duck, for they do not grope in the mud. Their bills are sharp and strong for fishing, and their wings long for flying. The little dabchick, on the contrary, has short wings, as he chiefly floats on the water. His beak is not very long, and it has no hook at the end. His feet are rather large, but the web is not wide as in ducks.

There are a great many other web-footed birds. Try if you can find some.

Examine a dead duck. Notice the webbed foot, the parts of the beak, the thick down, and the glossy oiled feathers not wetted in water. Draw the foot of any dead bird you can find.

CHAPTER XV: Bird Enemies

ALMOST every morning, when I wake, I hear a curious cry, "tek-tek-tek," in my garden, and I know that if I go out and look, I shall see the cat about somewhere. Sometimes many birds will be making the same cry all together, and when the cat is on the lawn I have seen the swallows swoop down and peck her back, and then rise up again before she can turn round.

For the birds know very well that the cat is their enemy, and scold at her when she comes near, especially when they have young ones.

I wonder if you have ever thought as you lie snugly in bed how many dangers there are for the little birds outside? The owl prowling along the hedge is on the look-out for sitting mothers and for young birds. The cat may climb the tree and put her sharp claws into the nest. Weasels and stoats are hunting about to catch any birds which are sleeping near the ground, or even in the trees, and snakes like eggs for their early breakfast as much as you or I do.

The fox is a great enemy of the ground birds. Partridges, pheasants, and grouse dread a fox at night, as the fowls and ducks do in the farmyard; while in the daytime the hawk is a terror to all birds. The mother lark, on her nest, crouches down in the hope that the grass may hide her. The father lark, as he soars, rises or falls to try to escape. Other little song-birds flutter away to the bushes; partridges run to cover, and pigeons hide in the wood when a hawk is near.

All these are the birds' natural enemies; for of course animals must kill their food, and we too kill birds to eat. But we need not destroy their nests nor take their eggs for show, nor catch them, as many do, in nets to put them in cages, or to use their feathers for ornaments.

STOAT HUNTING YOUNG ROBINS

Many birds, which were quite common thirty years ago, are rare now because such a number of eggs and birds have been taken. So laws have been made to protect the little song-birds, birds of prey, and sea-birds, as well as partridges and pheasants.

All over England people are now forbidden to shoot or snare *any wild birds* except on their own land, or to take their eggs, between the 15th of March and 1st of August. This leaves the birds time to bring up their little ones. And there is a special list of birds which people may not disturb, even in their own garden, during this "close time."

I am sure you will be glad to know that the lark is one of these birds.

Then there are some parts of England where people are not allowed to take the eggs of wild birds at any time. These are places, such as some of the Broads in Norfolk, and the sea-shore at Slapton Lee in Devonshire, where many birds breed.

You cannot know all these places, but there is one very safe rule. Do not take any eggs, nor kill any birds; then you are sure not to do wrong.

Watch the birds in the garden, and the fields, and the woods. Learn to know where they build their nests round your house, and take care they are not disturbed. When you wake up in the morning listen to their songs. You will soon know them, and know too when they are happy, or when something is frightening them. Then notice what good work they do, eating the slugs and snails, the wire-worms and grubs.

You must drive them away when you see them eating your seeds, or your young buds, or the sprouting corn. But you can feed them in winter to make them your friends, and you will be surprised how much you can learn about their ways.

Birds of the Air

Made in the USA
Coppell, TX
24 July 2022